I0437192

Promotional Mission Based Management

Management Theory

Rick Tresnak

DENVER, COLORADO

Promotional Mission Based Management
Management Theory
All Rights Reserved.
Copyright © 2013 Rick Tresnak
v2.0

Outskirts Press, Inc.
http://www.outskirtspress.com

ISBN: 978-1-4787-0227-6

Outskirts Press and the "OP" logo are trademarks belonging to Outskirts Press, Inc.

PRINTED IN THE UNITED STATES OF AMERICA

Contents

Chapter 1: Promotional 1
Chapter 2: Mission 11
Chapter 3: Base 17
Chapter 4: Management 25

Foreword

WE HAVE ALL worked in a society where money is the driving force, and corporations treat employees in a manner that is institutional. Fortunately we all know better we know right from wrong yet we still seem to fall into social norms creating for ourselves and environment of mistrust. Wouldn't it be much easier to just do things right and have others do things right as well. Yet we spend millions and millions of dollars on self-help books on management series that basically tell you the same thing just repackaged over and over again. But what we really need is someone to be a divine conscience for us.

Well a group of us set out to do just that. We wish to create a more utopian business model that can be utilized in any aspect of the market you are in. We first sat down and spent several months discussing what we don't like about our jobs and our career paths and how are employers treat us. After doing this it was evident that there were better ways of doing things and that greed and fear of law-suit were the two driving factors that created the environment we disliked.

One of our executives was driven out of the market that he was in as a business owner selling a leading cardiac monitor, because of restructuring they did not take his company into consideration. He was unable to sell his cardiac monitor to hospitals and ambulance services. This being completely ridiculous as where are you supposed to sell cardiac monitor. He struggled for several years trying to make ends meet selling AEDs to schools and law-enforcement agencies but due to the overabundance of these products in the market space is competition had grown significantly. Worse than that when he would land a big client the manufacturer would take the customer for themselves, leaving him with a very sour taste in his mouth. Ultimately they lost him as an employee.

I myself was a mid-level manager in a hospital system where my distrust had been well earned. Out of the blue one day I was pulled aside and reprimanded for apparently sleeping with an employee, well this had never happened but I wrote it off as a reminder not to place myself in situations where this may seem to be apparent. I was in charge of 60 employees in a department that wasn't making money, so upper management was always looking over my shoulder to determine what to do with the department. I wasn't given money and my budget to make improvements some of these critical to the success of the department. My future plans and goals for the department also were not taken seriously. This placed me in a very tight box. Without the needed changes it would be very difficult to increase the revenue stream and save the department. When I took over we were $187,000 in the red yearly. I had to be creative and think outside of the box in order to change that as quickly as possible.

It came down to education of the staff with new insurance laws and regulations. The way that we wrote our progress notes and our patient care reports had placed us in a situation where we were losing money despite our increased patient volume. After educating these people our income quickly improved. We went from $187,000 in the red to over $1 million in the black, quite the turnaround in one year. However this still did not allow for infrastructure changes in my budget, and I found out that I was not even being paid the same as other managers at the same level.

It was these types of corporate structure that bothered me. Out of control supervisors making split decisions, the yes-man mentality, the dog eat dog hierarchy and the complete lack of integrity were the driving factors after many years of torment drove me to becoming an entrepreneur. Other executives that I brought together to discuss this had several like experiences so we set out to create a company where these experiences would not be tolerated. Our first step in this process was to develop a management theory that not only fit our business model but that can fit any business model. We developed what we call promotional mission based management.

CHAPTER 1

Promotional

WELL THE GREATEST thing about promotional mission-based management is that it works in so many different arenas in so many different market spaces in any company model that has employees or customers. It takes the best of what we know as truth and makes it simple a management tool not full of fluff but just common sense. Let's look at it close break it down by its components can you tell me at the end of the book whether it can change your life.

Promotional is a focused effort achieving a positive result or advancement by raising the bar. Increasing or adding to. Developing.

So many times we are in a place where we can't excel because it's not part of the corporate structure and yet its own natural to try to do better for yourself. Let me ask you what makes a happy employee? A great work environment, opportunity for advancement, pay-for-performance, opportunity for intrinsic happiness, friendly environment not hostile environments, and benefits they provide for your family. Yet so many times we find ourselves missing key components of those things that we desire and this leads to retention issues poor customer service and loss of revenue. So let's change it!

I want you to think about the word promotional, think of it as a goal for you and your company. What goal do you set for your employees? Think of it as a chin up bar. If the goal is set at chest height for your employees so that they can easily reach their goal there is no advancement for them. In the same token if that push up bar was set 30 feet above them they would never be able to reach it causing resentment and frustration. The objective is to place the bar just of few feet out of reach so that when they reach that goal they actually accomplish something.

Because at chest level that push up bar is doing absolutely no good, it's too easy. Some employees feel comfortable doing mundane work however they're not the type of employee that you need working for you. The goal that you set for your company by looking at the word promotional should be set so as to jump to the occasion. Promotional isn't just for you and your employee, it's for you and your customers. How do you promote your customers? How do you make the experience that they have advantageous to them?

We'll take it from their point of view; they want a great product at a great price with timely delivery and some customer follow-up. But what sets your company apart from others? Everybody does that. Your company is going to be different! Because when you think of the word promotional you start thinking outside of the box. Let's say that your company sells tools and your customer walks in the door for the first time what do they see?

Are they meant by an employee that says hey how can I help you with excitement and energy or do they simply walk into a store and left on their own devices to find the product that they're looking for? That's simple fact that there's somebody there that's going to help them determine what tool they need and perhaps offer suggestions on how to complete their project increases that customer satisfaction. Is your store well laid out? Can they find what they're looking for? Are there small kiosks in the area where employees aren't looking at cell phones that are there to help?

What happens if that customer comes in and like most stores wanderers for 15 min. looking for somebody to help them, in a store that's poorly managed, has a poor lay out, and they are unable to find the product that they are looking for. Or worse they find the product with a price tag that is out of the market median. They will never come back into your store again. The let's change it up with some promotion. Imagine yourself being a customer walking into a store and having someone greet you. Wal-Mart has this right.

That little bit of caring at the front of the store sets the mood for their experience. You say hey I'm looking for a hammer can you show me where that is? The employee says sure and either takes you there themselves or gets an associate to help you. On the way over the employee engages conversation with you asking about the project that you are about to do. You say that you're building a deck for the first time. So the employee suggests not only a certain type of hammer but a book on deck building and a personal experience of their own. After only just a few minutes you found the perfect hammer have been led to several books and have made a personal connection with that employee. When you get to the checkout line there's somebody there that says how you found everything that you've come in looking for? Then the person hands you a slip of paper for 5% off the products that you have in your hand currently.

The reason that it is so important it's not you only get the 5% if you come back again. It's 5% off the purchase today! Now that 5% profit margin has already been built in to the price of a hammer and the book but feels to the customer like a great promotion. While there's that word promotion!

Let's look at the different business model, a church. You go into the church and you're met with a door greeter. It's your first time there and you've been given a tour of the facility. And you been now led to the sanctuary really you hear a great worship service with music the great sermon, and filled out a card for the church to contact you. This is pretty typical in churches today so what sets your church apart? So I tell you some things we can do to separate us from other churches. Every church looks the same there's pews or chairs the door greeter even the tour are the same. What happens if you change it up a bit? Instead of going straight into a church service you are introduced to a small group where they're standing around having coffee were sitting on couches nibbling on cookies and you been offered some. They get to know you and they start understanding why you're there. It's far less opposing; people can fit in small groups much easier than in large groups. It somebody taking notice of you then addressing your needs that keep people coming back. That church attendee has a much greater chance of returning to your church because somebody cares rather than the cold harsh reality of an institution.

In each of these cases be at a church or retail business somebody in the service industry your customers and employees deserve to be treated as if they mean something. They need to be promoted they need to be held up they need somebody to care. Sometimes they have grown into the mindset that they are not worth it. In order to retain great employees and great customers we have to leave them with the feeling that you're there to promote them.

Let's try and exercise. Imagine yourself walking into a car lot and in that car lot there are all sorts of cars and thinking about your salary in your waging your abilities pick out a car. Imagine yourself now with your new vehicle would like scratch that what's it like? Is it everything you've ever hope for in a new vehicle? I believe most of us don't believe that we are good enough to have the best vehicle. Now imagine your employee doing the same thing. What type of vehicle would that employee purchase? It's the same vehicle that your customer just purchased. How do we change this? Instead of buying a 1980 Chevy citation why aren't we buying the top-of-the-line product? What I want for you is for you to get the top-of-the-line product leather heated seats, sunroof, voice commands for air-conditioning, 26 airbags standard, chrome wheels, ground effects, the state-of-the-art sound system, and exterior the makes people turn their head. I want you to feel proud of the purchase that you just made. I want your employees to feel the same. I want your customers to be so ecstatic that their new purchase makes them cry from joy. That's what I want for my employees too.

Is it more important to have a customer come in once and make a large purchase worse quantity the way that we want to go? It's obvious we want our customers talk about our product about our company about our fine employees how they were treated with respect how they were assisted in their needs. That's promotion! By promoting these people we promote ourselves by setting the bar a little higher for them it sets the bar a little higher for us. Thinking outside of the box is essential to setting the goal. Now maybe you're not that creative but there are plenty of examples for you to follow in building success. Look at some of the most successful companies Disney for example says that the most important person in their company is the janitor. They encourage their employees to say hello to the janitors. That is promotion.

In our company we have strived to treat each other with respect. It has been a struggle at times but is been well worth it. Our turnover is low, but our dedication is high! We have set our corporate finances to reflect the employee's value. In our customers we've instilled confidence that we will give them quality service and great products at a reasonable price. We have gone so far in our commitment that we have searched out financial opportunities for our customers in order to purchase our higher-priced products. Opportunities like grants and low-interest loans help make this possible. Organizations that we do business with us also offer fund-raising opportunities. All of these things tell a customer that they are important to us. Our employees make a commission on each opportunity the customer takes advantage of in addition to their commission on the product.

CHAPTER 2

Mission

MISSION IS AN intrinsic direction of expelled energy to ward a calling. Assistance to those in need.

Mission is critically important to any company structure without this firm goal set in front of us we tend to flounder. How do you set your mission standards in front of your employees? It is something that is highly important for anyone of us to keep in mind. Let's first describe what a mission is. A mission is a goal or direction that has been laid down for us to follow to achieve a specific objective.

Can you imagine a soldier without a clear mission? Your troops would be in disarray, morale devastated, victory unobtainable and the loss of life tragic. Your mission has to be clear, well-defined so as to present the need and the goal. If you can perceive what you want then you can start to believe that you'll receive it. A mission isn't a simple idea or thought it should be a desire! Your mission should benefit mankind not just one small subculture. If you can impact the world with your mission and a positive manner even at a small level you have just done something remarkable! Missions are not supposed to be just corporate nature because if they are you are not promoting those outside of your organization. The organization would be set as the priority, whereas your customer base and your employees should be the priority.

A lot of corporations today are set up on pillars and these pillars are supposed to represent the attributes that your company feels are effective. But it doesn't set the goal in a clear and defined manner. Your employees and your customers could care less that you talk the talk instead of walking the walk. And they certainly cannot get behind your mission. If the desire that you have for your company is mixed with the determination of the people in your company and your customer base feels the benefit of your mission your company will never fail.

When we set out to have a utopian company one of the things we looked at rather deeply was the mission that we provide to the world. We looked at things that contributed to society and impacted communities that we are involved in as a whole. We will only bring on products that impact our communities in a positive manner. We will only offer services that we feel are beneficial to the communities we serve. We will create a culture of giving within the hearts of our employees to the communities they live in. If our employees view this with every customer interaction they will impact every customer they encounter in a positive way!

We look at ourselves from an environmental perspective as well we have a low carbon footprint. The way that we structure our company needs to be met with this in mind. So many companies today overlook this and yet negatively impact the world they live in. Look at all the different companies in the world that have embraced the environmental movement and have grown to great heights because of it. Customers want quality product at a reasonable price with great customer service and many of them want to do something good for the environment as well. Look at all the different companies that offer charitable contributions to the communities therein. While we do not openly advertise our charitable contributions we ask every employee to pick one charity they would like to support through our company. We then as a company reach out to that employee's charity and offer our assistance. This creates an environment where our employee feels good about the way they have impacted the world themselves. Imagine how your employee would feel if they were able to assist the charity of their choice and see the positive impact that has. Imagine how that employees spouse and children would feel. I'm sure pride would be one of the biggest emotions they would have.

It rolls back to promotion. By setting your mission in such a way that you strengthen that promotional feeling to your employee in your customer you win their heart we want to give back to the communities that were in so we are going to create an emotional experience. We want our employees to be a part of it. We want to impact the world through every customer relationship, and we want to impact every customer relationship with an employee experience. This is the portion where we engage the heart we empower those through the innovations that we sell we need to look at the needs before us and react in a fashion to best benefit those needs as a company. Sometimes this means looking beyond the balance sheet. But strangely enough our balance sheet doesn't suffer due to it.

There is a company called Newman's own Paul Newman is either the owner or the founder of this makes a claim on the front of the bottle of salad dressing the profits go to charity. Now I don't see that on other bottles on the store shelf yet Newman's own has a small line of products that obviously have a following. If what I say is true then Newman's own already knows this, they have their customer's heart in their hands.

CHAPTER 3

Base

YOUR BASE IS your character and your character needs to be developed.

The base of everything that we do this set on a preset determined set of norms and standards are brain has come to recognize as truth. Sometimes these norms and standards have been modified in undesirable ways by the society that we live in.

Have you ever studied hypnosis? Hypnosis is so simple it's crazy. To effectively hypnotize somebody you must first understand how the brain works. When we first start out in life absorbing all the information literally at our fingertips we start making assumptions on what we see on what we hear and what we feel to be true. We are creative thinkers because we have no preset boundaries that have been set for us. Santa Claus is real, the Easter Bunny delivers eggs, and your parents are superheroes. We take in input raw data in such a way that everything including magic exists. But as we grow older we start defining things most of the time through repetition and we develop a matrix that we use daily to determine fact from fiction.

Hypnosis is simply bombarding the mind from multiple directions with information that simply bypasses our matrix. Multitasking with more than five or six tasks is nearly impossible for the average human. Hypnosis takes advantage of this. By making the brain multitask it is easy to override the matrix and impregnate the brain with a new idea. I want you to think about how you view yourself. Think of a weakness or flaw. Can you not see that God created you in his likeness? So what has made you think that you have a flaw? It is probably been placed in your brain through creative advertising repetitive bantering from our society to make you think that! Recognize that we all have similar flaws and you start realizing that perhaps you are not alone but one of the norm. That means that that I deal person is truly the one that is flawed.

Your character has to be looked at from multiple angles to truly determine its reality in this world. When you look at your base you must determine first what you want your base to be. I personally wish to have high moral values, integrity, and a sense of loyalty. There are things in my character that I need to continually change to improve upon and to overcome. From a business standpoint I listen to the counsel of other executives before I listen to my own ideas on the matter. When people hear about an issue for the first time and have not given the proper thought many times they react in a knee-jerk fashion and most of the time it is an incorrect reaction. How we create our own base is a painstakingly difficult task at times. Others see your base daily and expect you to react in typical fashion time after time.

So let's look at your base and bring this concept all the way back to the beginning of this management tool, how does your base affect promotion. Is it in your character to help build up others? Is this something that you have given any thought to? Or is this something that society is shaped in you without your recognition? There is a term called autosuggestion it basically means having repetitive suggestions placed before you on a specific subject matter that will ultimately shape and guide your thought process. There are different people that have used it in positive manners such as dress for success, think yourself thin, and make yourself a better lover. (Laugh) but there are so many examples of how we react to others based on untruthful uses of autosuggestion.

Society uses autosuggestion to make people believe they have to be thin utilizing products that make them more attractive to the opposite sex and be successful in life. But when you look at it that's not how we were created we were each created differently and in different ways in if you do not embrace those differences in your company you lack the diversity and stagnate creativity. I have frequently pulled my staff aside and told them individually the reason that they were hired. I do this with the single purpose to promote their own self-image and to grow their confidence. I say things like your heart for customer service is so apparent in the way that you react to people that are the main reason that I have picked you for the job you are in. Knowing that person will embrace that comment I know the customer service will be something that they focus on.

This is a positive use of autosuggestion to effectively promote somebody else's base. It uses the principles of hypnosis in a unique way. First off by bombarding their brain with different streams of information and thought they become susceptible to autosuggestion. Let me explain when your boss comes up to you initially become self-conscious of what you're doing of the presentation of your environment that probably increases your thought process by 10%. Then to have your boss pull you aside typically increases anxiety adding at least another 5% more thought process into this equation. If I start my sentence by saying" I want to tell you what I think about you" this opens a door to near anxiety and panic. But then utilizing autosuggestion to inform them what I like about them that promotes them to think of their character or base in a better manner ultimately assists them in their mission.

I look for many positive examples in my life that shows me the flaws of my own character. None of these examples has been more effective than my faith. It seems that if I could take and harness all of my flaws listing them on a piece of paper and then matching each up with a positive example I could effectively prioritize my list and change my base. Our base is so important I met a man that was incredibly wealthy he had made his money and big oil then in being a bottom feeder. He would purchase companies to tear them apart and sell off their assets leaving countless numbers of people unemployed. Perhaps many of these companies were struggling financially but the disruption to the community was great. This man's character or base had to be completely flawed driven by greed and power seems to be the only two missions he had. Later in life he regretted his decisions and now strives to help companies overcome those same challenges that he faced in a positive manner. I likely would not have enjoyed this man's company and his early life but now I've grown fond of him all because he changed his character.

The way that our customers and our employees view our base and our character leaves a lasting impression on how they will interact with us in the future. If our character helps promote them ahead of us we will both grow but if our character only promotes us we stagnate. Our base affects our mission and our ability to promote others. I would like you to take a moment and on some paper write down your flaws no matter what they are and then ask yourself what has caused me to believe these are flaws. If you're honest with yourself you'll quickly see a trend the one that I've been speaking of. If you had been told all of your life that you are fat ugly stupid and that you would marry a loser you probably did and you want something better. Your employees and your customers are the same way. Assist them in thinking differently of themselves.

CHAPTER 4

Management

MANAGEMENT IS THE leadership of people in a system moving towards common goals.

Many people believe that management is something deserved I don't see it that way at all I see managers as leaders and leaders are born into it. I know there's many schools of thought on this theory the leadership can be taught but I believe that either you were a leader or you are a follower. Sometimes you've always been placed in a position where you are a follower and through some prodding and social development it may appear that you have been taught leadership. True leadership does take a sense of security in your own abilities to be effective but even the most uncommon leader can arise to an occasion. Overcoming personal fears has a lot to do with it. Like in the previous chapter your brain has been trained to react in a certain way through a series of examples that affect your leadership model. Your matrix has been developed in such a way that you react the way that others would react in a similar situation. But haven't you noticed that many times and corporation's positive moral values seem not to exist. Why repeat it?

If you are to take leadership and really break it down to its bare minimum you will find the leaders will either lead you away from danger or into danger. Some learn examples are positive some learn examples are negative here is the way to keep it separated. First ask yourself in this situation am I promoting the individual that I have encountered. Second does my decision work cohesively with my mission? Third does my decision in this situation match with my character strengths or flaws? If it matches with all three of these then chances are the decision that you make leads you away from danger.

Throughout this book I have tried to make it very simple. Doing the right thing every time that you possibly can too effectively change your community in a positive way is really a promotional mission-based management is all about. It can work in any setting whether it's in the business world or your home life. Simply by saying them I promoting those around me if I had a mission to make it better what would it be do I need to change something within myself to fulfill that mission and are my decisions are always based on those three things.

Why subscribe to this theory? By effectively changing the society that you are in we all reap the benefits and aspects that you influence. Your financial bottom line improves whether that's money or happiness. Your employees have a sense of community giving and belonging. Your employees have a sense of pride in the company they serve with. Your company reputation improves. Your customer satisfaction is built on brand loyalty. We help those in need and we lift up not only our customers our employees ourselves but our communities.

Many management books go into such depth over trivial things and they exclude the very basic practices of life they don't take into focus typically how to self-improve. But by understanding these simple practices and working at keeping those in the forefront of your business your company's success can be measured on multiple points of interest. Promotional mission-based management is our company's gift of promotion to you. We honestly hope and desire that you use it to develop a better workplace for yourself, and impact the communities that you interact with in a positive way. Never forget that each employee and customer has value far beyond your accountant's bottom line.

Promotional Mission Based Management is just a management theory that you can adopt to develop your organizations morale value. Several companies have adopted this theory and have been successful. I encourage you to at least give it some food for thought. Now I challenge you to go out and impact the world differently.